Con

Ready to go

Machines that help us to move from place to place are known as vehicles. Large vehicles, such as trains and ships, can move lots of people or goods in one go. Smaller vehicles, such as bicycles, may carry just one person at a time.

Vehicles can be used for fun as well as for travel.

Along the ground

The wheel was invented around 5 500 years ago, making it much easier to transport people and goods on land. Cars, buses and trains carry passengers from place to place. Other vehicles are designed for different jobs, such as carrying heavy loads.

Through the air

The first aircraft to carry people was a hot air **balloon**. Today's huge **airliners** can carry hundreds of people across the world in a single flight. Other aircraft hold just one or two people.

Space rockets can carry several people into space at once.

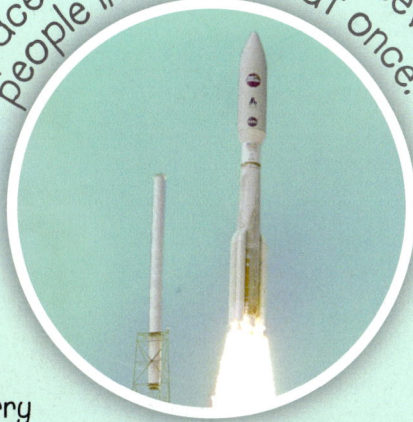

The Airbus A380 can carry up to 850 people. Its top speed is just over 1 000 kilometres per hour!

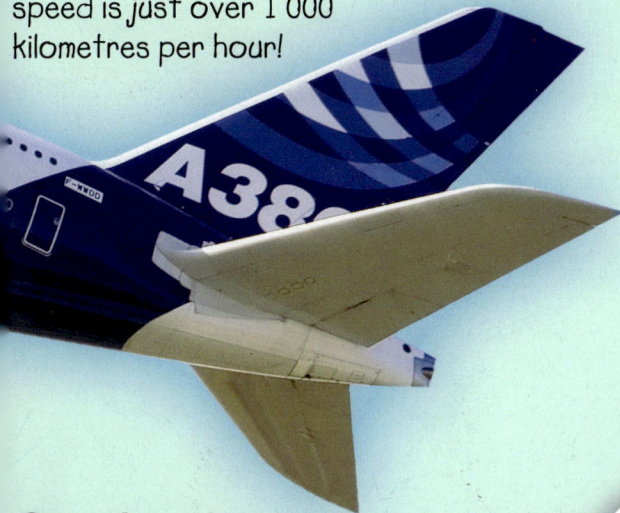

Over the water

The first boats were rafts made from logs. The Egyptians invented sails, helping boats to travel faster. Today, the biggest superships carry thousands of people on trips around the world. One- or two-person boats, such as dinghies, are used for fun.

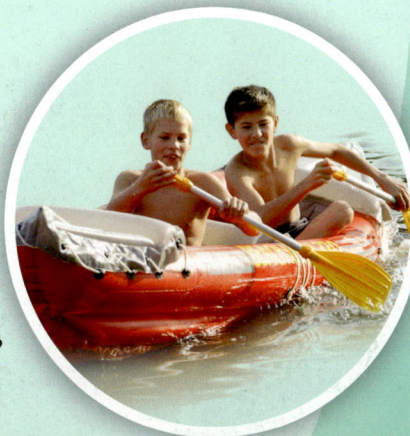

Choose your own journey

On some of the pages in this book, you will find coloured buttons with symbols on them. There are four different colours, and each belongs to a different topic. Choose a topic, follow its coloured buttons through the book, and you'll make some interesting discoveries of your own.

For example, on page 7 you'll find an orange button, next to a picture of a racing car. The orange buttons are about engine power.

engine power

There is a page number in the button. Turn to that page (page 15) to find an orange button next to a dump truck. Follow all the steps through the book, to find out how the different types of transport are linked.

science

safety first

people

Moving around

Vehicles are powered in many different ways. People or animals can push or pull small vehicles on the ground, or in the water. Boats can be pushed along by the wind. The largest vehicles have engines that help them to reach high speeds, and carry heavy loads.

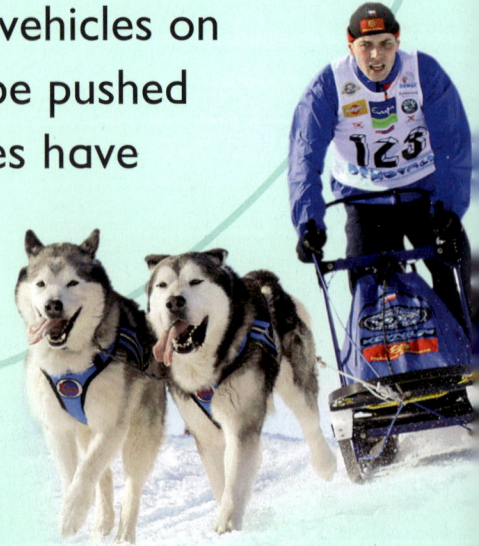

A cycle rickshaw carries schoolchildren through a city.

People ride in a cart attached to the bike.

Animal power

Carts, sledges and carriages can be moved by animals. People around the world still use horses, donkeys, oxen and dogs to pull these machines along the ground.

A cyclist turns handlebars to steer the bicycle.

Handlebars turn the front wheel left or right.

chain

pedal

People power

On a bicycle, the rider pushes the pedals around with his or her feet and legs. The pedals turn a chain, which turns the back wheel around. This moves the bicycle forwards.

Engine power

Motor vehicles have engines or motors to give them power. The engine turns the back wheel of a motorcycle. Cars, buses and lorries are motor vehicles too.

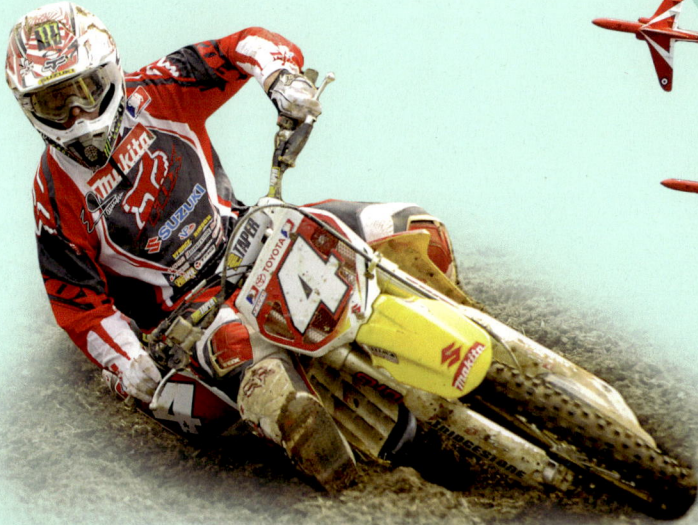

A motorcycle racer speeds along a muddy track.

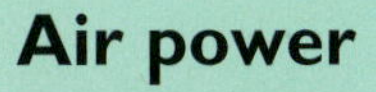

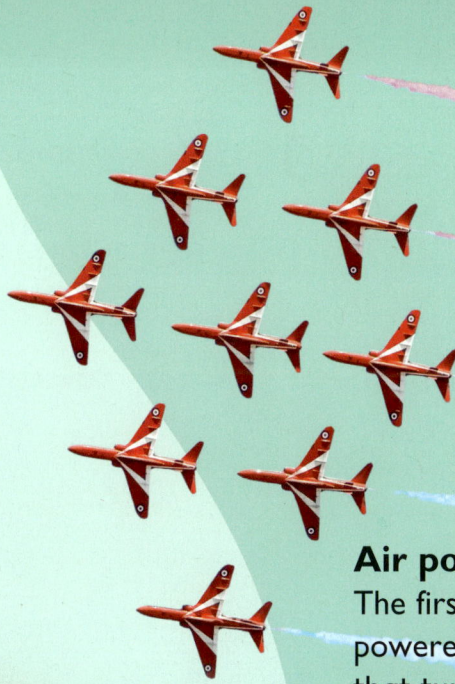

Air power

The first aircraft were powered by engines that turned **propellers**. Today, **jet engines** enable aeroplanes to travel faster and further.

Water power

Boats and ships float on rivers, lakes and seas. Some are powered by engines or by people pulling oars through the water. Others use the power of the wind to push them along.

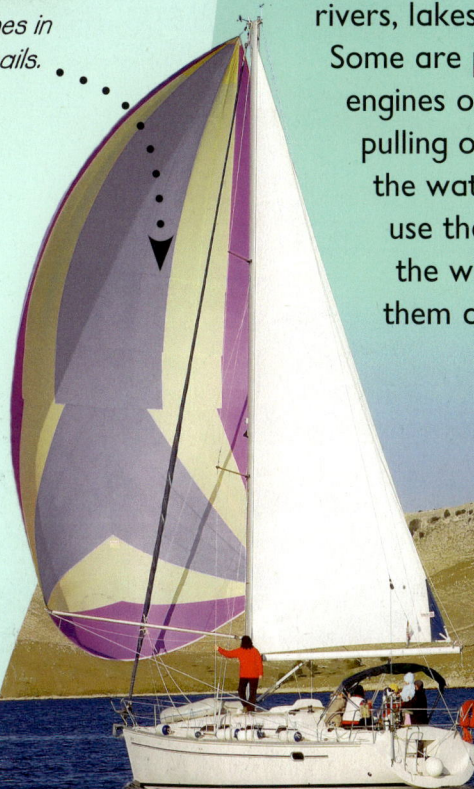

Wind catches in a yacht's sails.

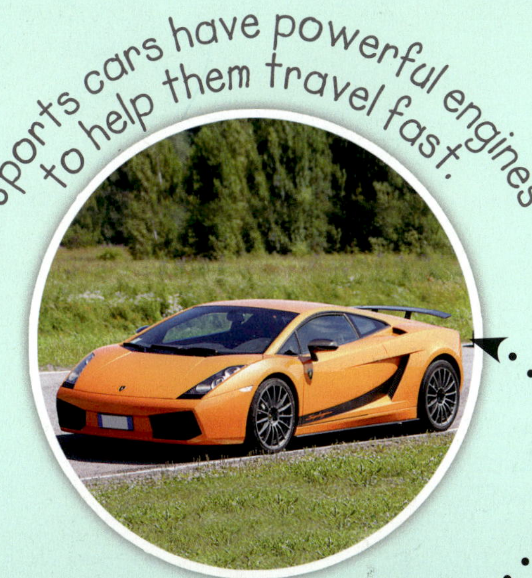

Sports cars have powerful engines to help them travel fast.

The engine in this car is at the back.

1 The crash barrier keeps crew and fans safe.

2 Mechanics change tyres in the pits.

3 A chequered flag signals the end of the race.

Racing vehicles have a smooth shape so that air flows easily around them. This is called streamlining. It helps vehicles to move forwards more quickly.

page 27

Daring racers

Ever since cars were invented, people have loved to race them. Today's Formula One racing cars are super-fast. They can reach up to 400 kilometres per hour – that's nearly four times the speed allowed on motorways! Thousands of fans gather to watch them race.

Drivers wear helmets and protective clothing.

5 Drivers brake and **accelerate** using pedals.

A Formula One car engine is very powerful. It allows the car to accelerate from sitting still to 200 kilometres per hour in less than 4 seconds.

page 15

Quick change

A Formula One race lasts for 60–70 laps of a twisting, turning track, called a **circuit**. If a car has a problem, the driver can steer it off the track and into the pit lane. There his team work quickly to fix the car or fit new tyres. Different tyres are used for wet and dry weather racing.

A strong harness straps a racing driver firmly into his seat. He wears a special suit that protects him from flames if there is a fire. A helmet protects his head.

page 18

Everyday journeys

A car is powered by an engine. The engine turns the car's wheels, driving the car forwards. The driver controls the car's engine using foot pedals. The accelerator pedal speeds the car up. The brake pedal slows the car down or stops it.

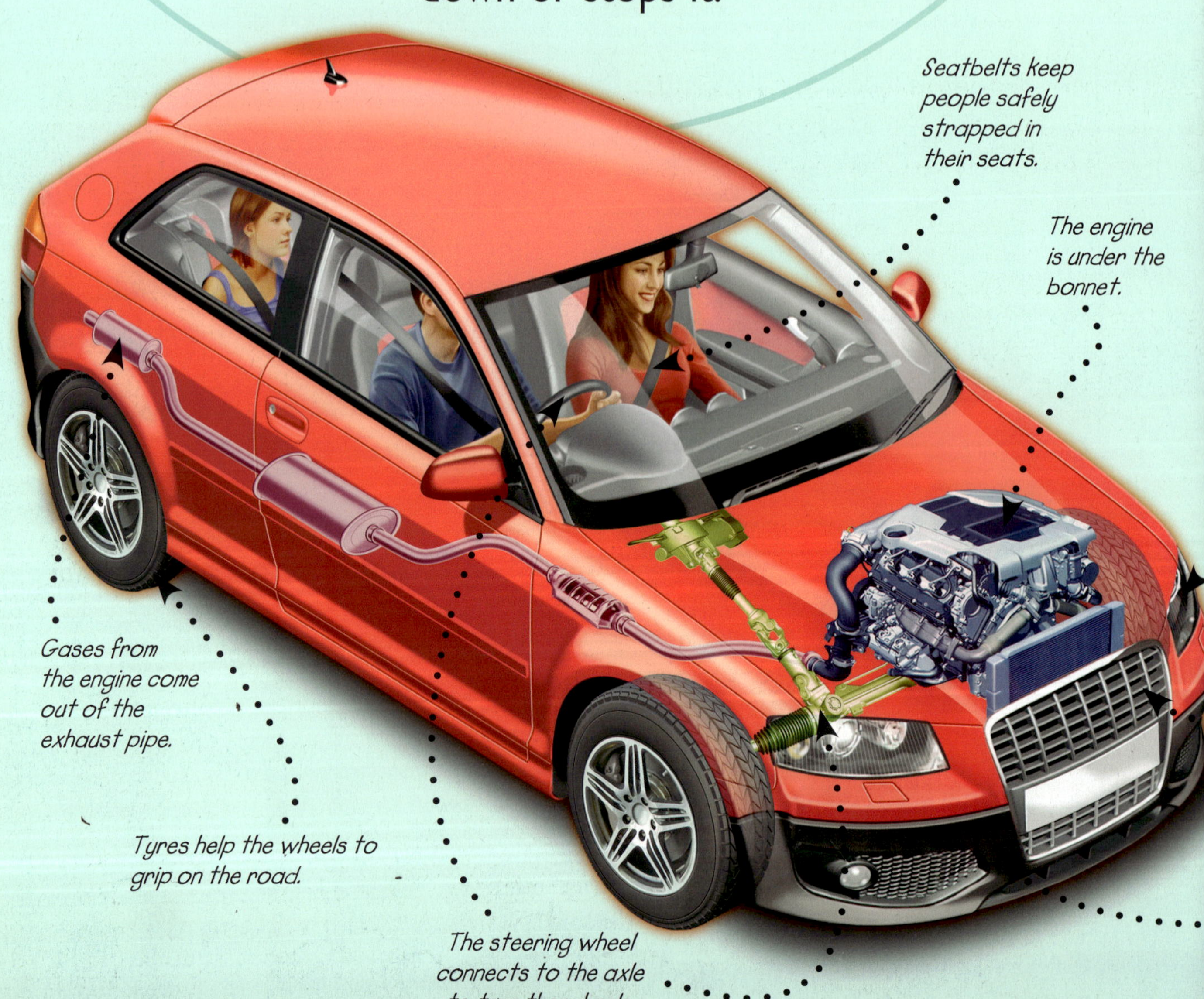

Seatbelts keep people safely strapped in their seats.
The engine is under the bonnet.
Gases from the engine come out of the exhaust pipe.
Tyres help the wheels to grip on the road.
The steering wheel connects to the axle to turn the wheels.

Starting the car
Turning the **ignition key** fires small sparks inside the engine and gets the car running. At the end of a journey, the driver turns the key again to stop the engine.

Drivers refuel their cars at a pump.

Fuel for energy
Most car engines work by burning **fuel** such as petrol or diesel This releases harmful gases which pollute the air. Some new cars have electric motors that run on battery power instead.

An electric car recharges its batteries.

How cars are made
Hundred of parts make up a modern motor car. The frame of the car is called the chassis. Other big parts, such as the engine, doors and **body panels**, are fixed to the chassis.

Mirrors help the driver to see what is behind the car.

Headlights light up the road ahead in the dark.

The radiator cools the engine down.

Bumpers protect the front and back of a car.

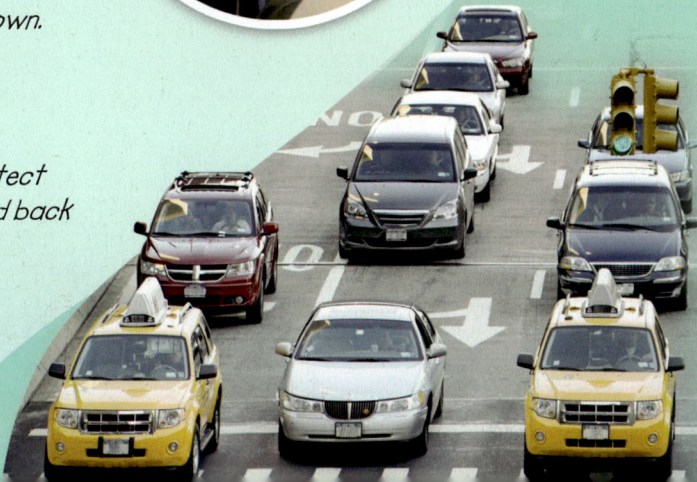

Cars travel on road networks that link many different places.

Staying safe
Roads are busy places so drivers have to pass a test to prove that they can drive safely. Signs warn drivers not to go over a certain speed. Signals such as traffic lights tell vehicles to stop to let other cars or people cross a road.

Transport in town

Every day, millions of people make journeys across towns and cities. Public transport vehicles, such as buses and trams, move lots of people in one go. They share the busy roads with bicycles, motorcycles and cars. Traffic signals keep passengers, drivers and **pedestrians** as safe as possible.

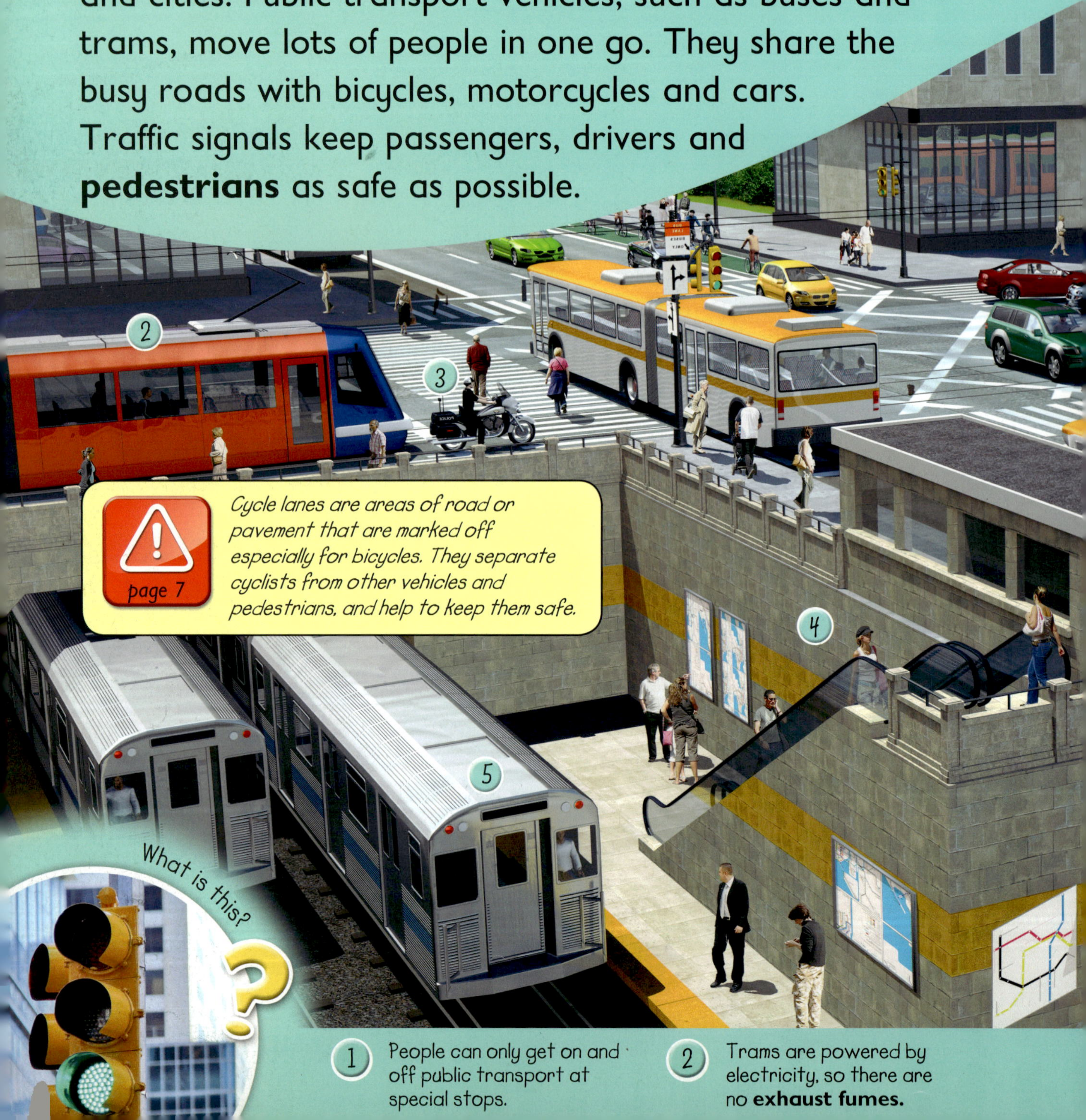

2

3

page 7

Cycle lanes are areas of road or pavement that are marked off especially for bicycles. They separate cyclists from other vehicles and pedestrians, and help to keep them safe.

4

5

What is this?

1 People can only get on and off public transport at special stops.

2 Trams are powered by electricity, so there are no **exhaust fumes.**

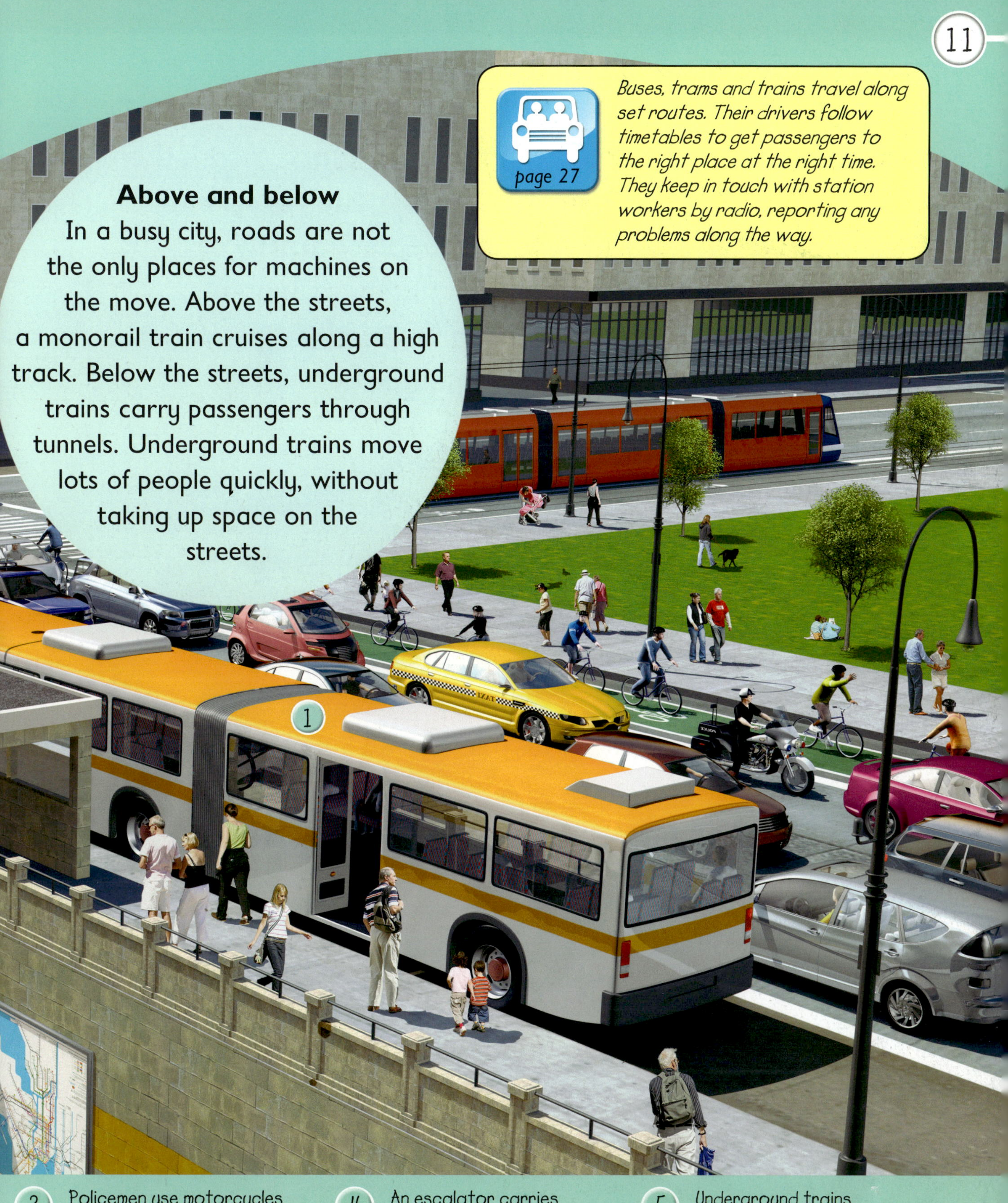

page 27

Buses, trams and trains travel along set routes. Their drivers follow timetables to get passengers to the right place at the right time. They keep in touch with station workers by radio, reporting any problems along the way.

Above and below

In a busy city, roads are not the only places for machines on the move. Above the streets, a monorail train cruises along a high track. Below the streets, underground trains carry passengers through tunnels. Underground trains move lots of people quickly, without taking up space on the streets.

3 Policemen use motorcycles to move quickly through traffic.

4 An escalator carries underground passengers quickly.

5 Underground trains avoid traffic jams on the streets.

On track

Trains run on railway tracks from one place to another. Their specially shaped wheels fit over the rails, keeping the train on the track. A **locomotive engine** at the front of the train pulls the carriages or wagons along. Locomotives can also push carriages from the back.

Steam power
Steam locomotives are powered by steam, which is made by burning coal to heat water in a big boiler. The steam pushes parts of the engine, making it turn the wheels round.

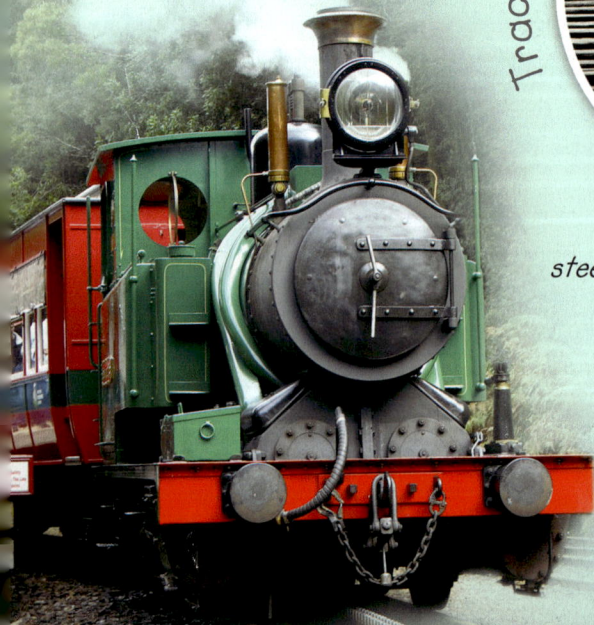

Tracks are made of long rails and shorter sleepers.

Underground trains have plen
of room for standing

Used steam escapes from the train's funnel.

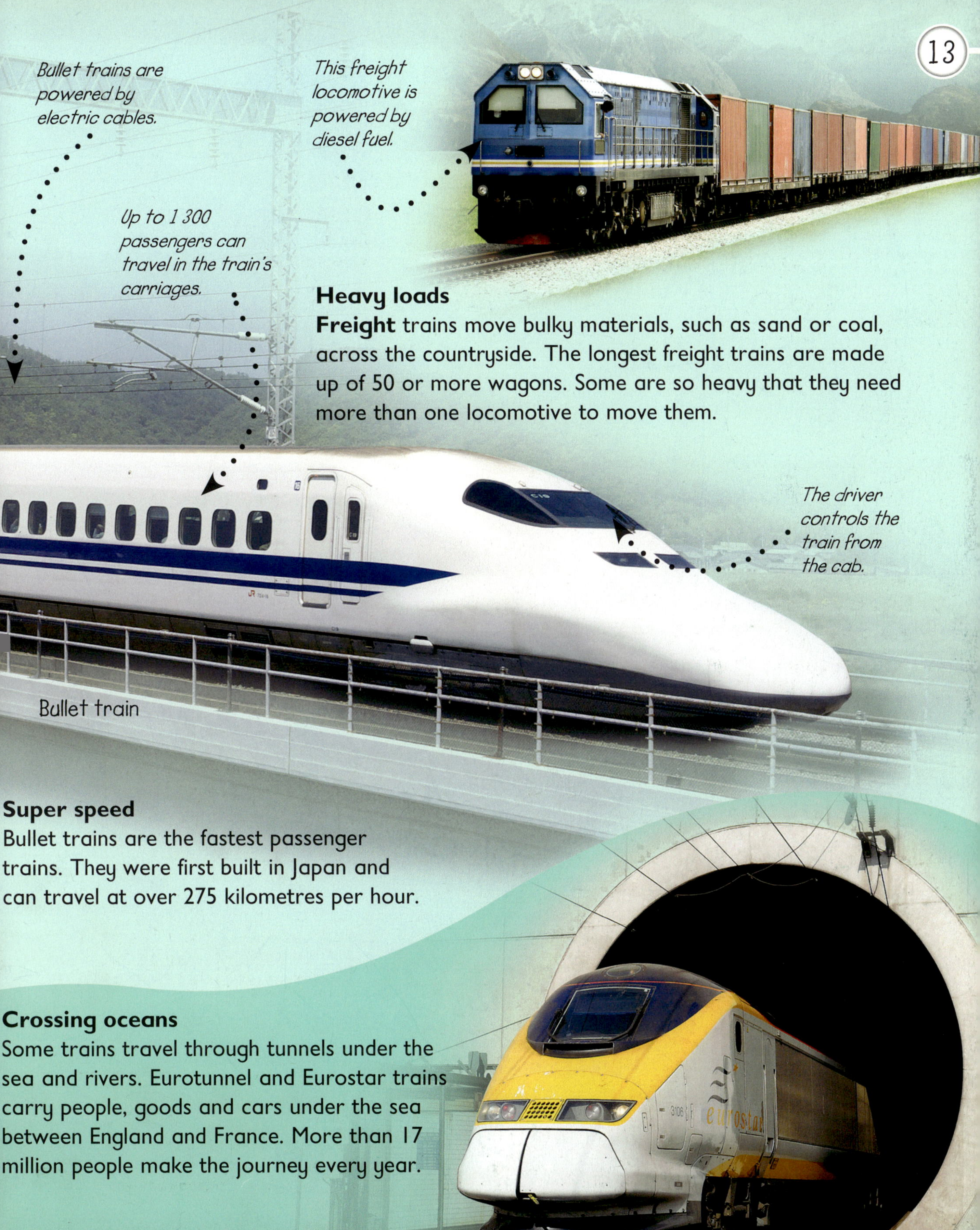

Bullet trains are powered by electric cables.
This freight locomotive is powered by diesel fuel.
Up to 1 300 passengers can travel in the train's carriages.
The driver controls the train from the cab.

Bullet train

Heavy loads

Freight trains move bulky materials, such as sand or coal, across the countryside. The longest freight trains are made up of 50 or more wagons. Some are so heavy that they need more than one locomotive to move them.

Super speed

Bullet trains are the fastest passenger trains. They were first built in Japan and can travel at over 275 kilometres per hour.

Crossing oceans

Some trains travel through tunnels under the sea and rivers. Eurotunnel and Eurostar trains carry people, goods and cars under the sea between England and France. More than 17 million people make the journey every year.

1 The cement mixer's drum turns to mix cement.

2 A flatbed truck delivers long girders.

3 A crane lifts heavy loads across the building site.

Heavyweight vehicles

Huge vehicles are used to move heavy loads on a building site. Trucks carry materials to the place they are needed. Fork-lifts, cranes and diggers move the materials around the building site. Cranes lift loads up high, while excavators reach low to dig **foundations**.

4 Fork-lift trucks can carry small but heavy loads.

5 Excavators are designed for digging.

6 A dump truck tips its trailer to deliver a load quickly.

7 A digger scoops up soil.

page 26

The world's largest dump trucks are over 15 metres long and 7 metres tall. Their giant engines give them power to carry up to 360 tonnes of rock – that is heavier than 50 adult elephants!

page 23

Caterpillar tracks are fitted to many heavy vehicles to stop them from sinking into soft or muddy ground. The tracks spread the weight of the vehicle over a larger area than ordinary wheels and tyres.

Jobs to do

Each vehicle has a different job. Trucks deliver **girders** and bricks, while other vehicles move them around the site. A dump truck delivers sand. Some of this will be taken to the **cement** mixer, where it will be churned with other materials to make cement.

Carrying heavy loads

Some vehicles are built to carry very large or heavy things. These machines have to be very tough. They need powerful engines so that they can transport their load – which may be heavy firefighting equipment, or even a house!

A moveable ladder lifts hoses up high.

This flatbed trailer carries a whole house.

Wide load

Articulated trucks have a driver's cab that can be fixed to different trailers. Some trailers are box-shaped and can hold goods inside. Flatbed trailers are flat with no sides, so large loads can rest on top.

A road train travels through Australia.

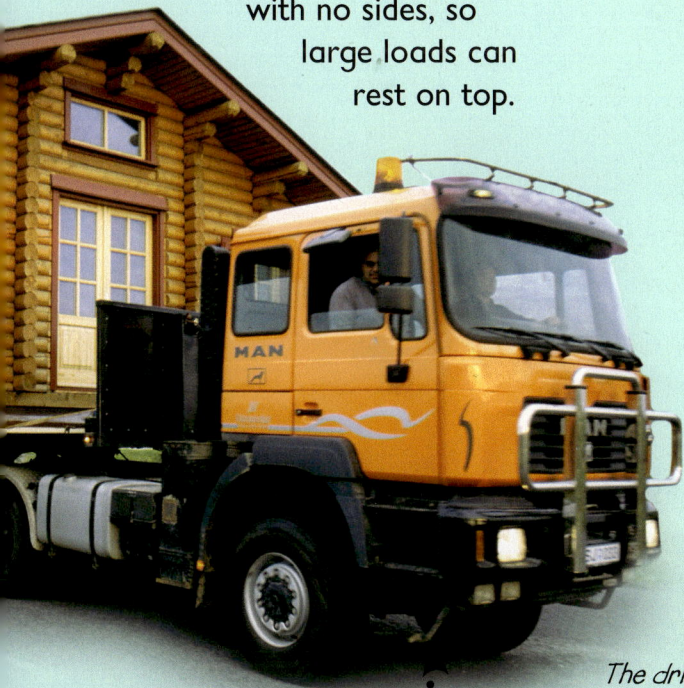

Coming through

Road trains have a powerful cab that can pull two, three or more trailers at once. They are used to transport things long distances, through areas with few towns.

Giant dump trucks are used in mining to move large loads of rock.

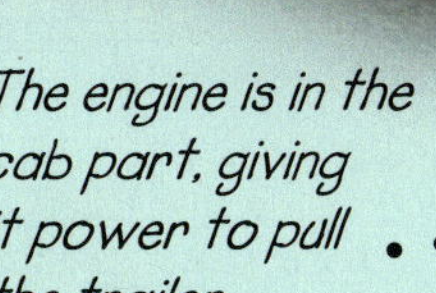

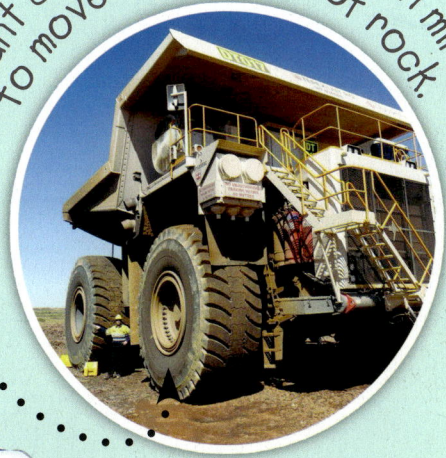

The engine is in the cab part, giving it power to pull the trailer.

The driver looks tiny next to these 3-metre wheels!

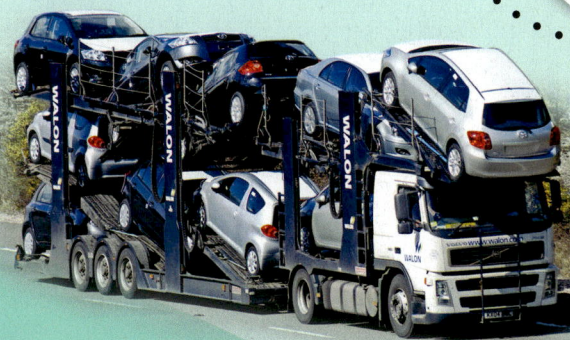

Carrying cars

Car transporters move cars from the factories where they were made to showrooms where they go on sale. The cars are driven on to the transporter and fixed securely in place.

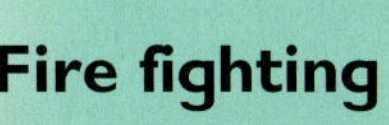

Fire fighting

Fire engines carry water, ladders, pumps and other firefighting equipment quickly to a fire. Their ladders stretch upwards to reach fires or rescue people trapped in tall buildings.

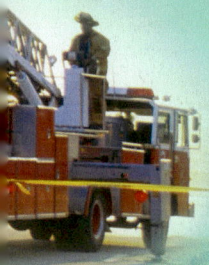

1 Ground marshals direct planes around the airport.

2 Landing wheels fold up once the plane is in the sky.

3 The pilot controls the plane from the cockpit.

page 22

Before a plane takes off, staff onboard carry out a safety demonstration. They show passengers what to do if there is a problem during the flight.

High fliers

Aeroplanes carry passengers and **cargo** all over the world, taking off and landing on **runways**. Airports often have more than one runway so that several planes can take off and land at the same time. On the ground, smaller vehicles help to transport passengers and their luggage around.

4 Platforms on lifts are used to load cargo on and off the plane.

5 People in the flight control tower tell each plane when to take off and land.

6 A windsock shows wind direction.

All aboard

Passengers are carried to their plane by bus. Their luggage is carried on a separate truck. The passengers board the plane using a mobile staircase, which is wheeled or driven up to the aeroplane door. When all the passengers and luggage are onboard, the plane **taxis** to the runway. The **air traffic controller** gives the go-ahead, and the plane speeds along the runway until it is travelling fast enough to take off into the air.

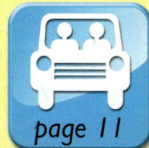

page 11

Air traffic controllers record the direction and height above the ground that aircraft are flying at. They talk to pilots using radios and help to guide them in to land safely.

Take-off

An aeroplane starts its journey by moving faster and faster along the runway. Air flows over the plane's wings, helping to lift it off the runway and up into the air. Giant jet engines give the plane power to speed along.

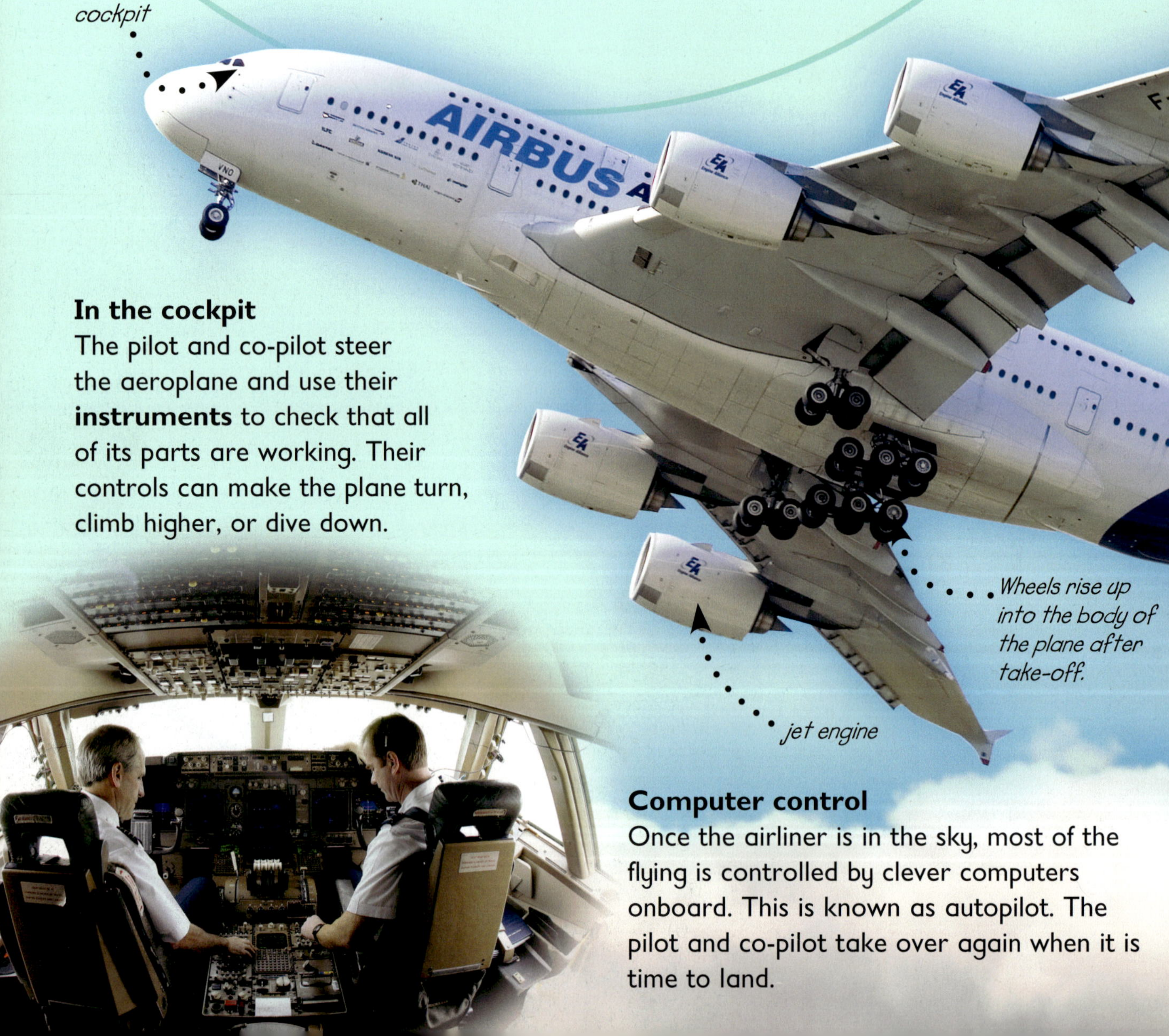

cockpit
AIRBUS
Wheels rise up into the body of the plane after take-off.
jet engine

In the cockpit
The pilot and co-pilot steer the aeroplane and use their **instruments** to check that all of its parts are working. Their controls can make the plane turn, climb higher, or dive down.

Computer control
Once the airliner is in the sky, most of the flying is controlled by clever computers onboard. This is known as autopilot. The pilot and co-pilot take over again when it is time to land.

Jet engines help fighter planes travel at high speeds.

Jet power
Large airliners have four huge jet engines, fixed underneath the wings. The jet engines **thrust** out hot gases, forcing the plane forwards.

Elevator flaps help the plane to fly up or down.

The body of a plane is called the fuselage.

Hot air balloons
A burner heats the air inside a hot air balloon. The warm air rises, carrying the balloon up into the sky.

Passengers ride in the basket.

Helicopters can hover in one place to rescue a person in trouble.

Rotor blades spin to let the helicopter hover in mid-air.

Water runway
Sea planes can take off from rivers, lakes and seas. Instead of wheels, they have large floats full of air, so the plane can rest on the surface of the water.

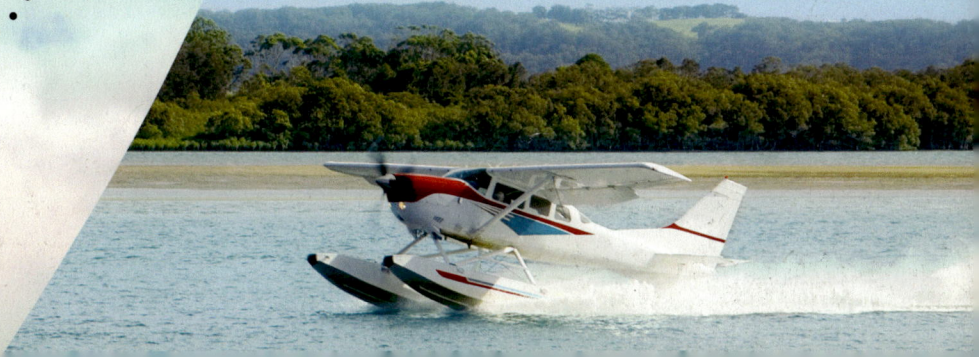

Riding the waves

Ships and boats have transported people and goods for thousands of years. People use boats for fishing, fun trips, and ferrying people and their cars across water. Larger ships carry passengers and cargo around the world.

What is this?

Many people wear lifejackets when they are travelling by boat. These are full of air or a very light material like foam, which floats well in water. Lifejackets help to stop people from sinking under the water if they fall in.

page 10

1 Sailing boats are powered by the wind's energy.

2 Boats like this fishing trawler are used to do work.

3 A tug boat tows larger boats in and out of harbour.

6

5

75632

ISABELLA

Coastguards help to keep everyone safe at sea. Sometimes they rush out of the harbour to help a boat or swimmer in trouble. At other times, they check on boat safety or act as policemen on the water.

page 19

Unloading

Most boats and ships sail in and out of ports or harbours, where they can transfer their loads to or from the land. Fishermen on a trawler unload their **catch**. A huge container ship unloads cargo. The coloured containers are lifted straight from the ship on to trucks or trains.

A rudder is a flat fin that is fitted to the back of a boat. It sits underwater and is used for steering. Pushing the rudder one way or the other changes the flow of water around the boat and helps it to turn.

page 6

4 Motorboats, like speedboats, are powered by engines.

5 The coastguard checks everyone is safe on the water.

6 Cranes unload giant containers full of goods.

Floating and diving

Boats and ships float on top of the water. Their specially-shaped bodies push the water away, and the water pushes back, keeping them above the surface. Boats must be carefully made so that they don't tip over or sink.

This rubber boat is filled with air.

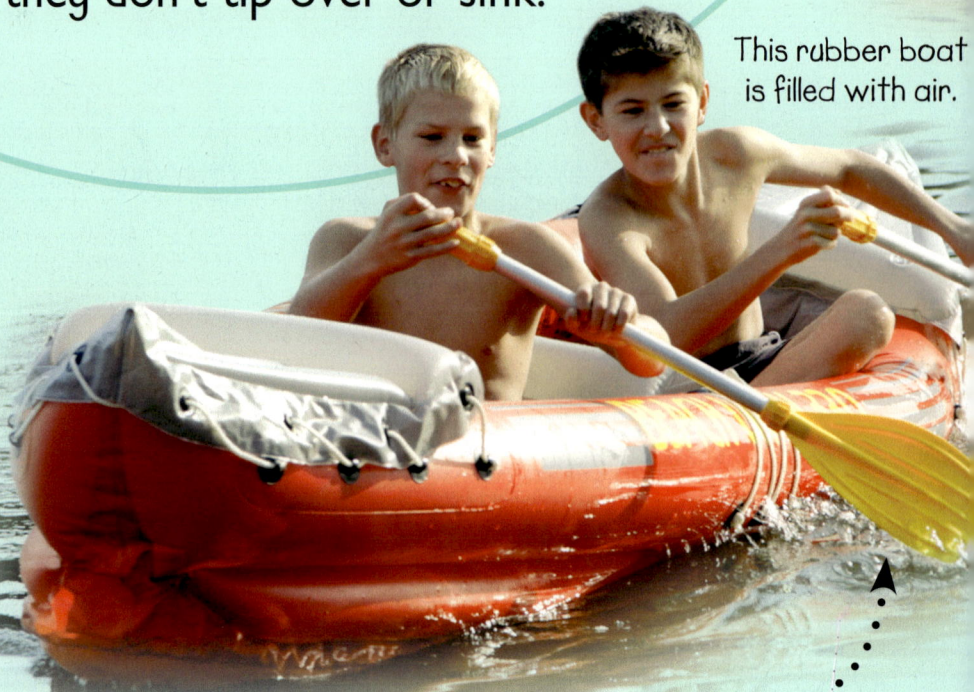

Staying afloat

Boats float because they are lighter than the water they push away. Some materials, like wood, float naturally. Other materials can be made to float by filling them with air. Air is much lighter than water, so the boat can carry people and still not sink.

Paddling pushes the water back, which moves the boat forwards.

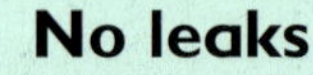

Amphibious vehicles can travel on both land and water.

wheels for use on land

No leaks

A boat's **hull** is made from tough materials like wood, steel or **fibreglass**. It must be **watertight** so that the boat doesn't sink.

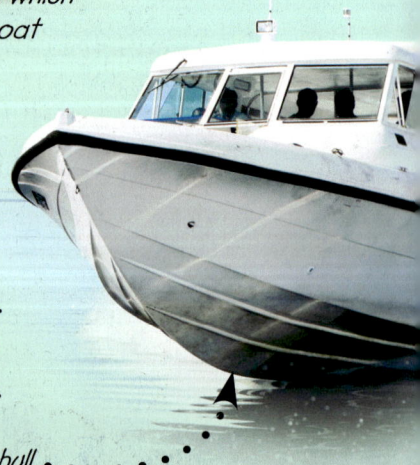

hull

A hydrofoil skims across the water.

front wing

A hovercraft "hovers" over water on a cushion of air

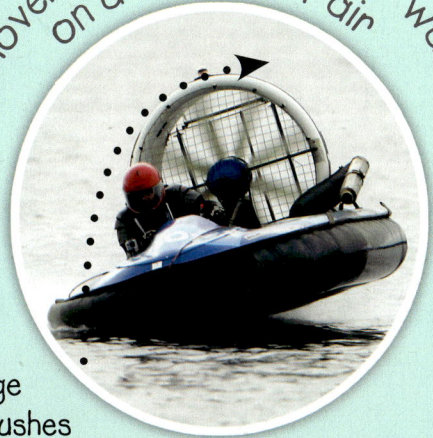

A large fan pushes the hovercraft forward.

Flying on water
Hydrofoils are boats with wings under the water. As the boat moves faster, the wings lift the hull up out of the water. This means the boat can skim across the surface very quickly.

Under the surface
Unlike other boats, submersibles travel underwater. They have tanks that can be filled with water to make them sink and dive down. The water is pumped out to let the submersible rise up again.

A glass dome gives amazing underwater views.

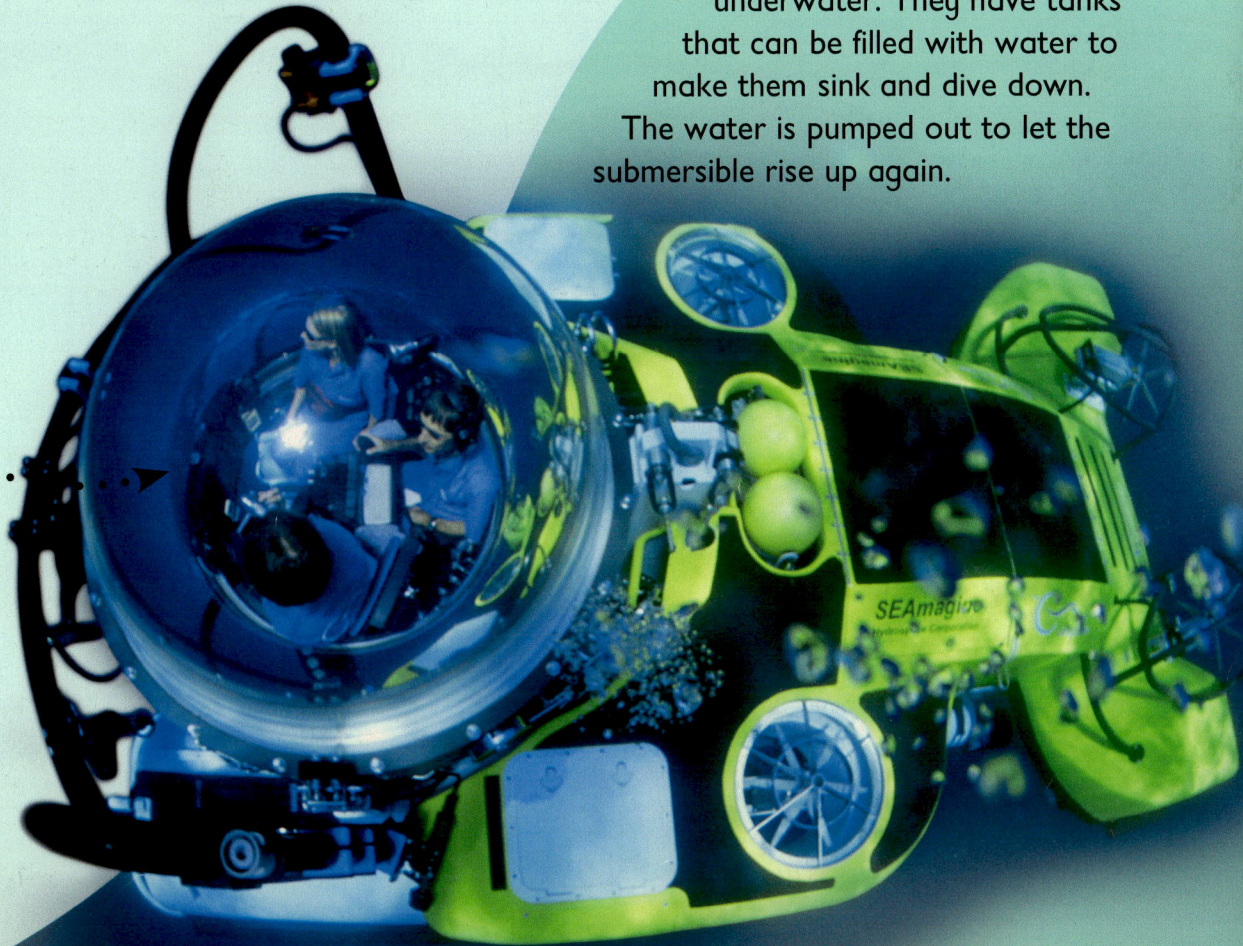

Rocket power

A space rocket blasts hot gases downwards to thrust itself up into the sky. The blast is enough to drive the rocket away from Earth, so it can carry its **payload** into space. This may be a **satellite**, astronauts on a space mission, or a spacecraft that will leave the rocket behind and travel far into space.

page 7

The engines of the Saturn V space rocket packed more power than 300 000 sports cars! Saturn V was as tall as a 36-floor building. From lift-off, it took just two and a half minutes to climb 68 kilometres into the sky.

1. A transporter carries the rocket to its launchpad.
2. The launchpad is hidden by gases from the exhausts.
3. The main rocket is over 40 metres tall.

Most rockets do not have astronauts onboard. Mission controllers stay on Earth but follow a space rocket's journey. They check that all goes well and can sometimes send radio signals to the rocket to change its course.

page 23

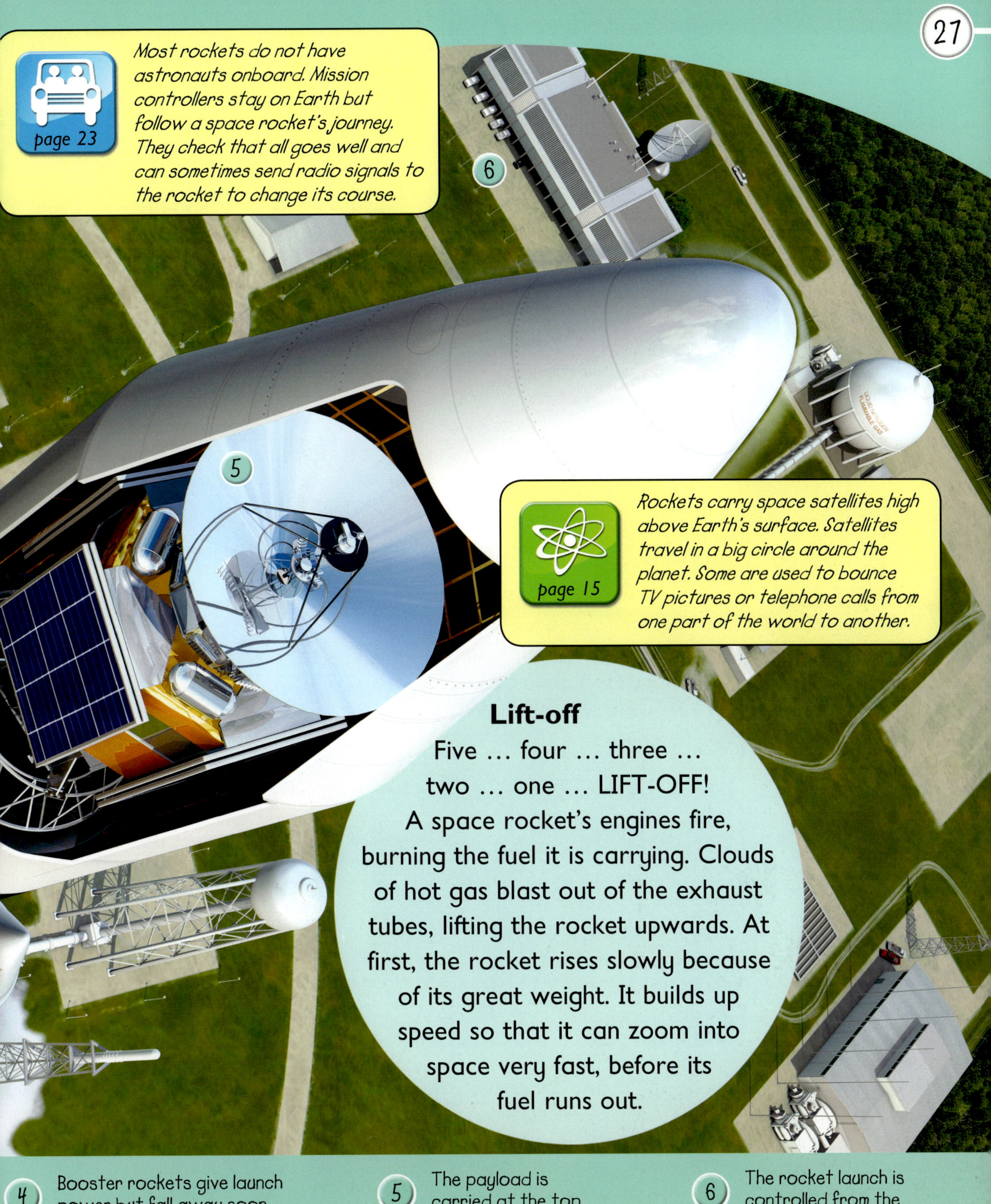

Rockets carry space satellites high above Earth's surface. Satellites travel in a big circle around the planet. Some are used to bounce TV pictures or telephone calls from one part of the world to another.

page 15

Lift-off

Five ... four ... three ... two ... one ... LIFT-OFF! A space rocket's engines fire, burning the fuel it is carrying. Clouds of hot gas blast out of the exhaust tubes, lifting the rocket upwards. At first, the rocket rises slowly because of its great weight. It builds up speed so that it can zoom into space very fast, before its fuel runs out.

4 Booster rockets give launch power but fall away soon after lift-off.

5 The payload is carried at the top of the rocket.

6 The rocket launch is controlled from the space centre.

Record breakers

Some people try to build machines that go faster than any before. These record-breaking vehicles need really powerful engines. They need smooth, sleek bodies to zoom through the air, water or space. They also need brave drivers!

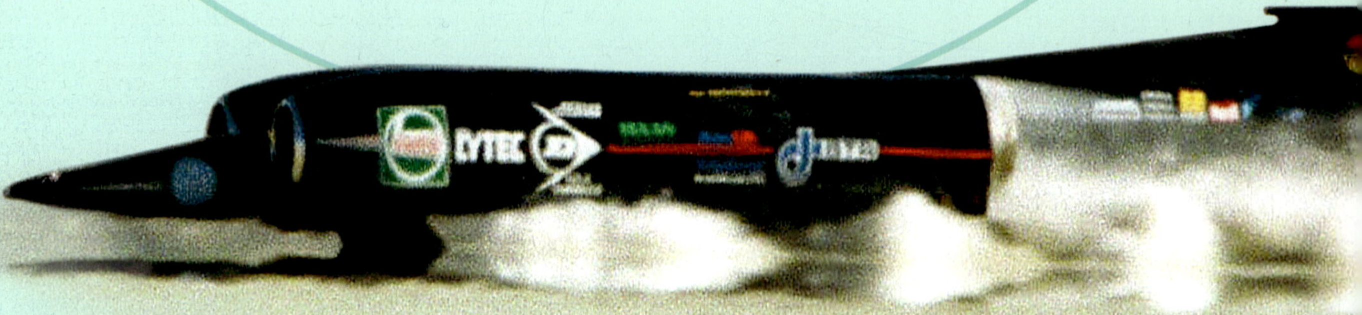

Land lightning

Thrust SSC is the world's fastest machine on land. In 1997, it raced along a flat desert and reached an amazing speed of 1 228 kilometres per hour. It was powered by two jet engines, normally used in fighter planes.

The fastest racing cars are called Top Fuel dragsters. These cars race in pairs along a straight piece of track. They finish their 400 metre-long race in less than five seconds.

A TGV train in France once travelled at
570 kilometres per hour.

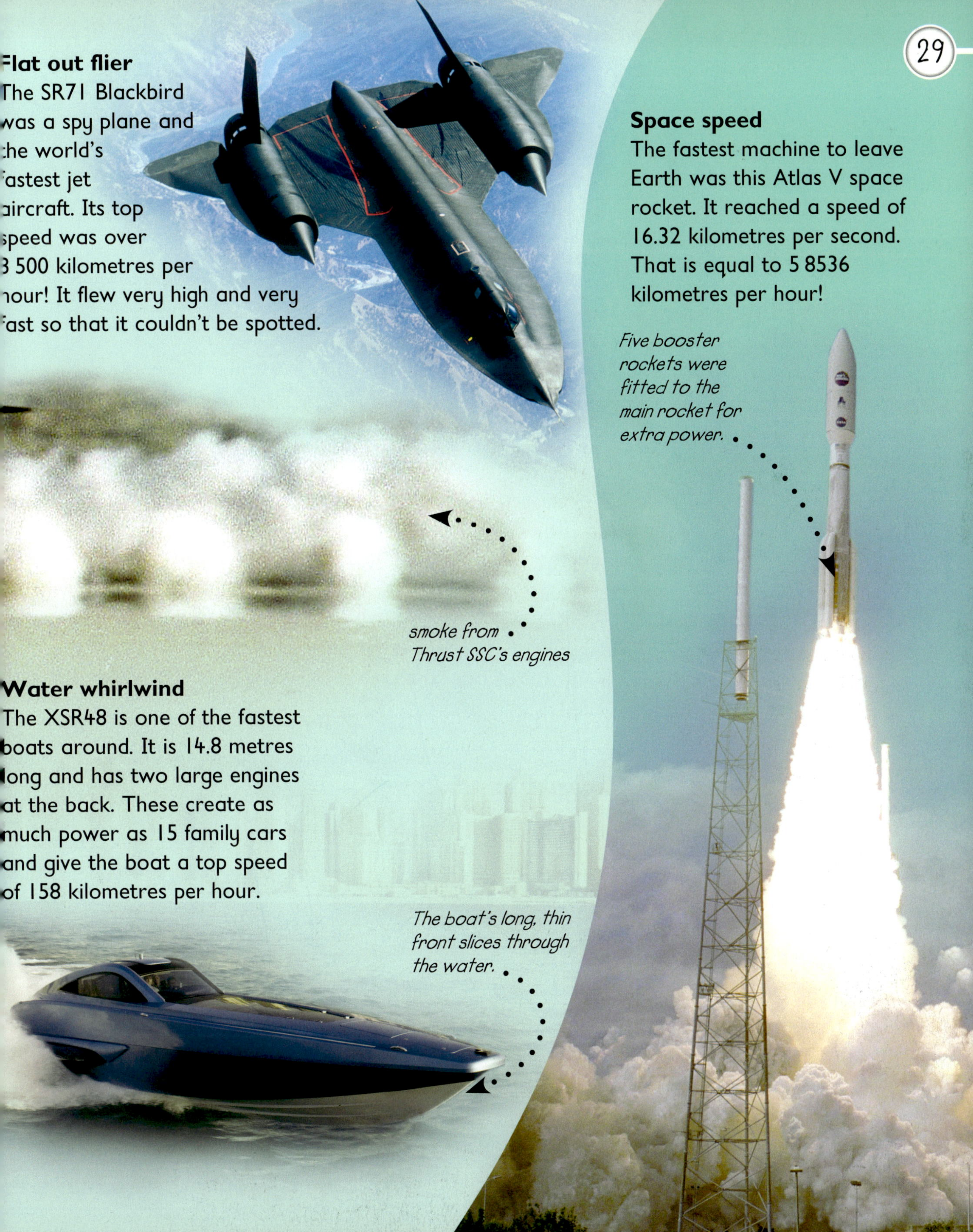

Flat out flier

The SR71 Blackbird was a spy plane and the world's fastest jet aircraft. Its top speed was over 3 500 kilometres per hour! It flew very high and very fast so that it couldn't be spotted.

Space speed

The fastest machine to leave Earth was this Atlas V space rocket. It reached a speed of 16.32 kilometres per second. That is equal to 5 8536 kilometres per hour!

Five booster rockets were fitted to the main rocket for extra power.

smoke from Thrust SSC's engines

Water whirlwind

The XSR48 is one of the fastest boats around. It is 14.8 metres long and has two large engines at the back. These create as much power as 15 family cars and give the boat a top speed of 158 kilometres per hour.

The boat's long, thin front slices through the water.

Glossary

accelerate increase speed

air traffic controller person who controls and monitors aircraft in a particular area

airliners large aeroplanes used to fly people from one place to another

body panels outside shell of a vehicle

cargo large amounts of goods

catch amount of fish caught

circuit route around an area

cement building material that becomes hard when water is added

exhaust fumes smoke or gas given off by an engine

fibreglass strong plastic material containing glass threads

foundations structure that hold up a building from beneath

freight goods carried by a plane, lorry or ship

fuel anything that is burned as a source of energy

girders heavy beams used to support a bridge or building

hull body of a boat

ignition key part that turns an engine on in a car or other vehicle

instruments tools used for special work

jet engines engines that causes forward movement by the power of a stream of gases being forced out in the opposite direction

locomotive engine engine that moves by its own power, used to push or pull trains

payload passengers, equipment or satellites carried by aeroplanes or rockets

pedestrians people who walk

propellers devices to make boats or small aeroplanes move forward

runways flat, smooth strips of ground where aeroplanes take off and land

satellite spacecraft that is sent into orbit around a planet

taxis travels slowly on the ground before taking off or after landing

thrust force that pushes a jet engine forward as it takes off

watertight constructed so tightly that water cannot get in

Quiz answers

pages 6–7 This is the steering wheel of a Formula One car. It is covered with buttons, which the driver uses to control the car.

pages 10–11 A traffic light shines green. This tells vehicles that they can move ahead.

pages 14–15 This is the tread on a truck's tyre, which helps it to grip the ground.

pages 18–19 This is a propeller. It spins round very fast and helps to power the plane through the sky.

pages 22–23 This is a boat's anchor. It is dropped to the seabed to hold the boat still.

pages 26–27 This is a group of exhaust tubes at the bottom of a rocket, where the hot gases blast out.

Index